DON'T LOSE *heart!*

COMPANION JOURNAL

BY MARY BETH WOLL, MA, LMHC
AND LINDA SMITH, BS

All Scriptures are quoted from the New International Version.

©2024 The Widows Project

All rights reserved. No portion of this book may be reproduced, stored in a retrieval system, or transmitted in any form or by any means—electronic, mechanical, photocopy, recording, scanning or other—except for brief quotations in critical reviews or articles, without the prior written permission of the authors.

ISBN paperback: 978-1-7362169-6-5

David Woll: Cover Design
Kristi Knowles: Interior Layout/Design

Don't Lose Heart! Journal

Don't Lose Heart! has a very definite purpose and goal—to offer you healing support during your grieving process. We want to help you recover from your devastating loss so you can move forward into a life of effectiveness for God, becoming fruitful; even 30, 60, and 100 times more productive than you ever were before! (Mark 4:20).

We have designed this journal to be used as a companion to *Don't Lose Heart! A Widow's Guide to Growing Stronger.* Each chapter has a Growing Stronger Guideline with an accompanying life principle and Scripture.

How to use this journal:

Each week, as you prepare for and meet with your *Don't Lose Heart!* group, we have provided space in your journal for:

1. Study notes,
2. Meeting notes, and
3. Further reflection.

We wrote this book and journal because we care about you! We have been where you are now. We pray that God will bless you with His love and comfort as you grow stronger in your *Don't Lose Heart!* journey.

With love and prayers,

Mary Beth and *Linda*

Mary Beth Woll, MA, LMHC
Linda Smith, BS

GROWING STRONGER GUIDELINE #1

KEEP FIRST THINGS FIRST

Develop an intimate relationship with Jesus
because you are powerless to overcome grief
in your own strength.

*"The Spirit of the Sovereign Lord is on me, because the Lord
has anointed me to preach good news to the poor"
(Isaiah 61:1, NIV).*

Study Notes

Meeting Notes

Further Reflection

GROWING STRONGER GUIDELINE #2:

DON'T SUFFER ALONE

Give your Broken Heart to God and His People
to Receive healing from both.

*"The Spirit of the Sovereign Lord is on me...
He has sent me to bind up the brokenhearted"
(Isaiah 61:1).*

Study Notes

Meeting Notes

Further Reflection

CONNECTION LEADS TO FREEDOM

To become truly healed, share your story with safe,
significant others as well as with Jesus.

*"The Spirit of the Sovereign Lord is on me ... to proclaim
freedom for the captives and release from darkness
for the prisoners" (Isaiah 61:1).*

Study Notes

Meeting Notes

Further Reflection

THROW OFF EVERYTHING THAT HINDERS

With God's help, get rid of It!

"Therefore, since we are surrounded by such a great cloud of witnesses, let us throw off everything that hinders and the sin that so easily entangles, and let us run with perseverance the race marked out for us" (Hebrews 12:1).

Study Notes

Meeting Notes

Study Notes

Meeting Notes

Further Reflection

Growing Stronger Guideline #6:

Hang in There

Whenever you feel like giving up, endure.

"Let us fix our eyes on Jesus, the author and perfecter of our faith, who for the joy set before him endured the cross, scorning its shame, and sat down at the right hand of the throne of God" (Hebrews 12:2).

Study Notes

Meeting Notes

Further Reflection

Growing Stronger Guideline #7:

Don't Lose Heart!

When you experience discipline, remind yourself that God is a good Father and say, "My Abba (Daddy) Father loves me."

"No discipline is enjoyable while it is happening—it's painful! But afterward, there will be a peaceful harvest of right living for those who are trained in this way" (Hebrews 12:11).

Study Notes

Meeting Notes

Further Reflection

Growing Stronger Guideline #8:

Don't Grow Weary

Remember that your victory is just around the corner.

*"Therefore, strengthen your feeble arms and weak knees.
Make level paths for your feet, so that the lame may
not be disabled, but rather healed" (Hebrews 12:12–13).*

Study Notes

Meeting Notes

Further Reflection

GROWING STRONGER GUIDELINE #9:

REMEMBER THAT GOD IS ON YOUR SIDE

God's love is not based on your performance,
but on His goodness.

*"The Spirit of the Lord is on me...to proclaim the year
of the Lord's favor and the day of vengeance of our God"
(Isaiah 61:2).*

Study Notes

Meeting Notes

Further Reflection

GROWING STRONGER GUIDELINE #10:

DO NOT GRIEVE ALONE

Weep with those who weep until God,
Himself, wipes away all your tears.

*"The Spirit of the Lord is on me...to comfort all who mourn,
and provide for those who grieve in Zion—to bestow on them
a crown of beauty instead of ashes, the oil of gladness instead
of mourning, and a garment of praise instead of a spirit of
despair" (Isaiah 61:2b–3).*

Study Notes

Meeting Notes

Further Reflection

GROWING STRONGER GUIDELINE #11:

LET YOUR LIGHT SHINE

Grow stronger through your loss
and become a blessing to others.

*"They will be called oaks of righteousness, a planting of the
LORD for the display of His splendor" (Isaiah 61:3b).*

Study Notes

Meeting Notes

Further Reflection

Growing Stronger Guideline #12:

Invest in the Future

When you glorify God through your grief, you become
an example that will encourage generations to come.

*"They will rebuild the ancient ruins and restore the places long
devastated; they will renew the ruined cities that have been
devastated for generations" (Isaiah 61:4).*

Study Notes

Meeting Notes

Further Reflection

Milton Keynes UK
Ingram Content Group UK Ltd.
UKHW051329070724
445033UK00006B/90

9 781736 216965